Published By Adam Gilbin

@ Ryan Beal

Zone Diet: 100+ Fast and Delicious Recipes for Breakfast, Lunch, and Unlocking the Secrets of Weight Loss

All Right RESERVED

ISBN 978-87-94477-67-3

AF107571

TABLE OF CONTENTS

Quinoa And Vegetable Stir-Fry 1

Greek Salad 3

Goya Champuru 5

Buckwheat Pancakes Topped With Unsweetened Applesauce And Cinnamon: 7

Quinoa And Vegetable Breakfast Burrito 9

Sardinian Whole Grains Bread With Olive Oil 11

Nicoyan Black Beans And Rice 14

American Chop Suey With Salad 17

Antipasto Salad 20

Fennel, Apple, And Celery Salad 23

Espagnol Sauce 25

Seasoned With Smoky Paprika 27

Excellent And Healthy 29

Grilled Chicken With Fresh Herbs 30

Baked Salmon With Lemon And Rosemary 31

Stir Fry Tofu With Mixed Vegetables 34

- Spicy Minced Chicken With Mango 37
- Chicken Summer Rolls 39
- Vanilla Strawberry Doughnuts 42
- Sausage Breakfast Casserole 44
- Lentil Soup 46
- Baked Salmon With Lemon And Dill 48
- Umibudo, Additionally Referred To As Sea Grape Salad 50
- Rafute Miso 52
- Goya Chanpuru Tofu, Or "Sour Melon And Tofu Stir-Fry" 53
- Spinach And Feta Cheese Muffins: 56
- Overnight Oats With Almond Milk, Chia Seeds, And Sliced Peaches: 59
- Ikarian Herb Omelette 61
- Vegetable Scramble 64
- Arroz Con Pollo 68
- Chicken Stir Fry 70
- Baby Spinach And Strawberry Salad 72
- Eggplant Caviar 74

Dill Sauce 76

Brazilian Tilapia Stew 78

Bella Buns With Tuna Burgers 81

Scrambled Eggs With Spinach And Tomatoes 84

Tuna Salad With Chickpeas And Cherry Tomatoes 86

Turkey Burger With Guacamole 88

Grilled Polenta With Ham & Asperagus 91

Noodles With Chicken & Brussel Sprouts 93

Egg With Baby Spinach 95

Frittata 97

Sweet Potato And Black Bean Tacos 99

Grilled Chicken 101

Shima Rakkyo 103

Goya Miso 105

Somen Chanpuru 107

Sweet Potato Hash With Bell Peppers, Onions, And A Poached Egg: 110

Brown Rice Cake With Almond Butter And Sliced Strawberries: 112

Whole Grain Waffles With A Side Of Greek Yogurt And Fresh Fruit: 113

Adventist Breakfast Burrito 115

Japanese Miso Soup And Tofu 119

Baked Avocado Chicken And Vegetables 122

Bbq Salmon & Brussels Orzo 125

Baked Chicken And Broccoli Salad 126

Cottage Cheese With Tomato & Guac........................... 129

Cottage Cheese Snack 130

Warm Shrimp Salad... 131

Chicken And Applesauce Burgers.................................. 132

Duck Breast With Cranberry Sauce 135

Omelette With Mushrooms And Low Fat Cheese........ 138

Quinoa Salad With Chickpeas And Feta 141

Quinoa And Vegetable Stir-Fry

Ingredients:

- 1 zucchini, sliced
- 1 cup broccoli florets
- 1 cup snap peas
- 2 tablespoons low-sodium soy sauce
- 1 tablespoon rice vinegar
- 1 cup quinoa
- 2 tablespoons olive oil
- 1 onion, sliced
- 2 cloves garlic, minced
- 1 red bell pepper, sliced
- Salt and pepper to taste

Directions:

1. Cook quinoa according to package Directions:.
2. In a large pan, heat olive oil over medium heat.
3. Add onion and garlic, and sauté until fragrant.
4. Add red bell pepper, zucchini, broccoli, and snap peas. Stir-fry for 5-7 minutes, until vegetables are tender-crisp.
5. In a small bowl, whisk together soy sauce and rice vinegar.
6. Add cooked quinoa and the soy sauce mixture to the pan with vegetables. Stir well to combine.
7. Season with salt and pepper to taste.
8. Serve hot.

Greek Salad

Ingredients:

- 1/2 cup Kalamata olives
- 1/2 cup crumbled feta cheese
- 2 tablespoons extra-virgin olive oil
- 1 tablespoon lemon juice
- 1 teaspoon dried oregano
- 2 cups mixed salad greens
- 1 cucumber, diced
- 1 cup cherry tomatoes, halved
- 1/2 red onion, thinly sliced
- Salt and pepper to taste

Directions:

1. In a large salad bowl, combine mixed greens, cucumber, cherry tomatoes, red onion, Kalamata olives, and feta cheese.
2. In a small bowl, whisk together olive oil, lemon juice, dried oregano, salt, and pepper.
3. Drizzle the dressing over the salad and toss gently to coat.
4. Serve immediately.

Goya Champuru

Ingredients:

- 2 minced garlic cloves
- A serving of soy sauce
- Mirin (sweet rice wine), 1 tbsp
- 1/fourth cup of cooking oil
- 1 deseeded and thinly sliced sour melon (goya)
- 1 cubed piece of firm tofu
- Half a cup of optionally sliced beef
- Thinly sliced, half of an onion
- Pepper and salt, as preferred

Directions:

1. Soak the bitter melon slices in water with a touch of salt for 10 minutes in a basin.

Bitterness is lessened as a result. Drain, then set apart.
2. Heat the frying oil over medium-high heat in a huge pan or wok.
3. Upload the sliced pork and sauté it, if using, till it starts to brown.
4. Include sliced onions and chopped garlic. Stir-fry the onions till they're transparent.
5. Include the bitter melon slices and tofu cubes within the pan.
6. Whisk together the soy sauce and mirin, then pour the combination over the meals within the pan.
7. Continue to stir-fry for a few more minutes to completely cook the tofu and sour melon.
8. To flavor, add salt and pepper to the dish. Serve hot with steamed rice.

Buckwheat Pancakes Topped With Unsweetened Applesauce And Cinnamon:

Ingredients:

- Unsweetened applesauce for topping
- 1 cup buckwheat flour
- 2 tablespoons coconut sugar or sweetener of your choice
- 1 teaspoon baking powder
- 1/4 teaspoon salt
- 1 cup almond milk (or any milk of your choice)
- 1 tablespoon melted coconut oil or butter
- Ground cinnamon for sprinkling

Directions:

1. In a bowl, whisk together the buckwheat flour, coconut sugar, baking powder, and salt.

2. Add the almond milk and melted coconut oil or butter to the dry Ingredients:. Stir until just combined.
3. Heat a non-stick skillet over medium heat and lightly coat it with cooking spray or a small amount of oil.
4. Pour 1/4 cup of batter onto the skillet for each pancake.
5. Cook until bubbles form on the surface, then flip and cook until golden brown.
6. Stack the pancakes on a plate.
7. Top with unsweetened applesauce and sprinkle with ground cinnamon.
8. Serve warm.

Quinoa And Vegetable Breakfast Burrito

Ingredients:

- 1/4 cup diced onions
- 1/4 cup black beans, drained and rinsed
- 1/4 cup shredded cheese (such as cheddar or Monterey Jack)
- Whole wheat tortillas
- 1/2 cup cooked quinoa
- 2 large eggs, scrambled
- 1/4 cup diced bell peppers
- Optional toppings: salsa, avocado, Greek yogurt

Directions:

1. In a skillet, sauté the bell peppers and onions until they are softened.

2. Add the cooked quinoa and black beans to the skillet. Stir to combine.
3. Push the quinoa and vegetable mixture to one side of the skillet and add the scrambled eggs to the other side. Cook the eggs until they are fully cooked and scrambled.
4. Mix the scrambled eggs with the quinoa and vegetable mixture.
5. Warm the whole wheat tortillas in a separate skillet or microwave.
6. Spoon the quinoa and vegetable mixture onto the tortillas.
7. Top with shredded cheese and any optional toppings.
8. Roll up the tortillas to form burritos and serve.

Sardinian Whole Grains Bread With Olive Oil

Ingredients:

- Sardinian whole grain bread (or any whole grain bread of your choice)
- Extra virgin olive oil
- Sea salt (optional)

Directions:
1. Select the Bread: Start by choosing a good-quality Sardinian whole grain bread, if available.
2. Whole-grain bread is rich in fiber and nutrients, making it a healthier choice. However, you can use any whole-grain bread that you prefer.
3. Slice the Bread: Using a sharp knife, slice the bread into thick, rustic slices. You can make them as thick or thin as you like, but a hearty thickness is recommended.

4. Toast the Bread: You can prepare this dish by either toasting the bread or leaving it untoasted, depending on your preference.
5. Toasting will give the bread a delightful crunch, while untoasted will maintain its natural softness.
6. Drizzle with Olive Oil: Place the slices of bread on a serving platter or individual plates.
7. Drizzle extra virgin olive oil generously over the bread. The rich, fruity flavor of the olive oil is a key element of this dish, so don't be shy with it.
8. Sprinkle with Sea Salt (Optional): If you like, you can sprinkle a pinch of sea salt over the olive oil.
9. This adds a subtle savory touch that complements the olive oil's richness.
10. Serve: Your Sardinian Whole Grain Bread with Olive Oil is ready to be served. It's a simple yet delightful dish meant to savor the natural

flavors of the bread and olive oil. Enjoy it as a snack, appetizer, or alongside other Mediterranean-inspired dishes.

Nicoyan Black Beans And Rice

Ingredients:

- 2 cloves of garlic, minced
- 2 tablespoons of vegetable oil
- 1 teaspoon of ground cumin
- Salt and pepper to taste
- 1 cup of black beans (dried or canned)
- 1 cup of long-grain white rice
- 2 cups of water
- 1 small onion, finely chopped
- Fresh cilantro for garnish (optional)

Directions:

1. Prepare the Beans: If using dried black beans, soak them overnight in cold water.

2. Rinse and drain them before cooking. If using canned beans, rinse them thoroughly and drain.
3. Cook the Rice: In a medium-sized saucepan, combine the white rice and 2 cups of water.
4. Bring to a boil, then reduce the heat to low, cover, and simmer for about 15-20 minutes or until the rice is cooked and the water is absorbed. Remove from heat and let it sit covered for an additional 5 minutes.
5. Saute the Onion and Garlic: While the rice is cooking, heat the vegetable oil in a separate skillet over medium heat.
6. Add the finely chopped onion and minced garlic. Saute them until they become soft and translucent.
7. Add the Beans: Stir in the black beans and ground cumin with the sauteed onion and garlic.

8. Cook for an additional 5-7 minutes, allowing the flavors to meld together. Season with salt and pepper to taste.
9. Combine Rice and Beans: Once the rice is cooked and the beans are flavored, combine the two in a serving bowl.
10. Mix them together gently, ensuring that the beans are evenly distributed throughout the rice.
11. Garnish and Serve: If you like, garnish your Nicoyan Black Beans and Rice with fresh cilantro leaves for a burst of color and flavor.
12. Enjoy: This hearty and nutritious dish is now ready to be enjoyed. It's a staple in Nicoya, Costa Rica, and can be served as a satisfying main course or as a side dish with other Latin American-inspired dishes.

American Chop Suey With Salad

Ingredients:

- 1/2 (14.5 oz) can diced tomatoes
- 1/4 tsp crushed red pepper flakes
- 1/2 cup lettuce
- 1/8 red bell pepper
- 1/4 cup cucumber
- 1 tbsp fresh-squeezed lemon juice
- 1 tbsp water
- 1 tsp dr. Sears' zone extra virgin olive oil
- Iin 1/2 cup zone pastarx fusilli
- Cooking spray
- 1 oz extra-lean ground turkey breast
- 1 clove garlic (minced)

- 1/4 tsp basil (dried)
- 1/2 celery stalk (chopped)
- 3 tbsp onion (diced)
- 3 tbsp red bell pepper (diced)
- 1 tbsp water
- Salt and pepper (to taste)

Directions:

1. Cook Zone PastaRx Fusilli as directed. Drain and set aside.
2. Meanwhile spray a skillet with cooking spray and sauté turkey, garlic and basil until no longer pink.
3. Add celery, onion, peppers and 1-2 tablespoons of water, cook for a few minutes.
4. Stir in the cooked Zone fusilli.
5. Top with canned tomatoes and crushed red pepper. Stir well and cover and simmer for about 8 minutes.

6. Make a small side salad with the lettuce, red bell pepper and cucumber. Dress with lemon juice and water mixture.

Antipasto Salad

Ingredients:

- 1 cup onions - in half rings
- 2 1/4 cups red bell peppers - in half rings
- 3/4 cup garbanzo beans - canned
- 2 oz chunk light tuna in water
- 2 oz low-fat part-skim mozzarella cheese - shredded
- 3 oz sliced turkey - julienne
- 2 oz extra-lean ham slice - julienne
- 2 tsp dried basil - crushed in the palm of your hand
- 3 tsp dr. sears' zone extra virgin olive oil - drizzle
- 1 1/2 heads iceberg lettuce - shredded

- 2 cups celery - sliced
- 3/4 cup carrots - sliced thin
- 3 cups mushrooms - sliced
- 1/4 cup no-fat tasty dressing

Directions:
1. On three large oval plates arrange a bed of lettuce on each plate.
2. Place on the bed of lettuce, starting in a vertical line from the right side of the plate to the left, celery, carrots, mushrooms, onions, red pepper and garbanzo beans.
3. Then place the tuna, cheese, turkey and ham on the plates divided with strips of red bell pepper.
4. Crush the basil in the palm of your hand to release freshness and sprinkle over each plate.
5. Drizzle a teaspoon of extra virgin olive oil on each plate.

6. Whisk the No-Fat Tasty Dressing and pour over salads.

Fennel, Apple, And Celery Salad

Ingredients:

- 2 tsps water
- To taste salt and pepper
- 8 oz bulb of fennel (half pound, thinly sliced, including some of the feathery tops)
- 1 apple (thinly sliced)
- 2 celery stalks (thinly sliced)
- 2 tbsps lemon juice
- 1 1/2 tsps dr. Sears extra virgin olive oil
- 1 tbsp low fat feta cheese

Directions:

1. Whisk together lemon juice, olive oil, water, and salt & pepper in a medium bowl. This will make the dressing.

2. Toss with remaining Ingredients:.

Espagnol Sauce

Ingredients:

- 1 tsp dried parsley flakes
- 1 tbsp red wine
- 2 tsps garlic - minced
- 1/8 tsp dried oregano
- 10 tsps cornstarch
- 3 cups kitchen basics unsalted beef stock
- 1/8 tsp worcestershire sauce
- 1/2 cup tomato puree
- 1/3 cup onion - finely diced
- salt and pepper - to taste

Directions:

1. Combine all ingredients in a small saucepan to form a sauce. (Mix cornstarch with a little cold water to dissolve it before adding to saucepan.)
2. Heat sauce to a simmer, constantly stirring with a whisk until mixture thickens.
3. Transfer sauce mixture to a storage container.
4. Let cool and refrigerate.

Seasoned With Smoky Paprika

Ingredients:

- 1/4 teaspoon caraway seed
- 2 tablespoons smoked paprika, or to taste
- 1 tablespoon Worcestershire sauce, or to taste
- Pepper to taste
- 1 tablespoon cornstarch mixed with 1/4 cup water
- 1 tablespoon fresh basil, chopped
- 3 teaspoons olive oil
- 8 ounces choice veal, cubed to 1/2-inch pieces
- 3 cups diced onion
- 2 cups tomato puree or crushed tomatoes

- 6 cloves of garlic, minced (or to taste)
- 2 cups low-fat beef stock
- 1 cup cauliflower mash per serving (Recipe below)

Directions:

1. Preheat the oven to 400 degrees. Coat the bottom of a 2-quart casserole dish with the olive oil.
2. Combine all the Ingredients:, except the cornstarch mixture and the basil, in a bowl and stir together well; transfer the mixture to the coated casserole dish.
3. Cover the dish tightly with foil and cook for 20 minutes in the oven.
4. Remove the casserole from the oven; add the cornstarch mixture and the basil. Stir well; return the casserole to the hot oven and cook another 10 minutes, covered tightly.
5. Serve over cauliflower mash.

Excellent And Healthy

Ingredients:

- 2 teaspoons olive oil
- 2 cups salsa, any variety, pre-prepared
- 12 ounces of white fish, 6-ounces per serving
- 4 cups cooked snow peas, 2 cups per serving

Directions:

1. Preheat the oven to 375 degrees. Spread the olive oil in the bottom of a baking dish.
2. Place the fish fillets in the dish, turn over once and top with the salsa. Cover the baking dish tightly with foil and bake the fish for 20 minutes or until it will flake easily with a fork.
3. Serve the fish on top of the snow peas.

Grilled Chicken With Fresh Herbs

Ingredients:

- 1 clove garlic, finely chopped
- Fresh herbs (rosemary, thyme, parsley) to taste
- Salt and black pepper
- 150g skinless chicken breast
- 1 teaspoon olive oil
- Lemon juice (optional)

Directions:
1. Preheat grill to medium heat.
2. In a bowl, mix the olive oil, minced garlic, chopped fresh herbs, salt and pepper.
3. Rub the chicken breast with the herb mixture, making sure it is evenly covered.

4. Place chicken on preheated grill. Cook for about 6-8 minutes per side or until the chicken is completely cooked. You can test for doneness by lightly slicing the chicken and making sure the juices are clear.
5. While cooking, you can brush the chicken with a little lemon juice if you want a touch of freshness.
6. Once cooked, remove the chicken from the grill and let it rest for a few minutes before carving.
7. Serve the grilled chicken with low-carb vegetable sides or a green salad to keep your blocks on track.
8. This recipe offers a delicious way to enjoy the juicy flavor of grilled chicken while staying Local. Adjust portions based on your personal nutritional needs.

Baked Salmon With Lemon And Rosemary

Ingredients:

- 1 teaspoon olive oil
- 1 thin slice of lemon
- 1 sprig of fresh rosemary
- 150g of salmon fillet
- Salt and black pepper

Directions:
1. Preheat the oven to 200°C.
2. Place the salmon fillet on a sheet of aluminum foil lightly greased with olive oil.
3. Brush the salmon with olive oil and add salt and black pepper to taste.
4. Place the lemon slice on top of the salmon and place the fresh rosemary sprig on top.
5. Close the aluminum foil around the salmon, forming a kind of "package".

6. Place the salmon packet on a baking sheet and bake for about 15 to 20 minutes, or until the salmon flakes easily with a fork.
7. Once cooked, gently unroll the package, being careful of any hot steam that may escape.
8. Transfer the salmon to a platter and serve with side dishes of leafy greens or quinoa to maintain nutritional balance.
9. This baked salmon recipe is rich in protein and offers a delicious mix of fresh flavors thanks to lemon and rosemary. Customize portions to your individual nutritional needs.

Stir Fry Tofu With Mixed Vegetables

Ingredients:

- 1 teaspoon fresh ginger, grated
- 1 cup julienned mixed vegetables (carrots, peppers, courgettes)
- 1 tablespoon low-sodium soy sauce
- 1 teaspoon rice vinegar
- 1 teaspoon honey or maple syrup (optional)
- Toasted sesame seeds for garnish
- 150g extra-strong tofu, drained and cut into cubes
- 1 teaspoon sesame oil
- 1 clove garlic, finely chopped
- Salt and black pepper

Directions:

1. Press the tofu between two towels to remove excess water. Cut it into cubes.
2. In a nonstick skillet, heat the sesame oil over medium-high heat.
3. Add the cubed tofu and cook until golden on all sides.
4. Add the minced garlic and ginger to the tofu and cook for about a minute.
5. Add the julienned vegetables to the pan and cook for a further 3-5 minutes until tender but still crunchy.
6. In a small bowl, combine the soy sauce, rice vinegar, and, if desired, honey or maple syrup.
7. Pour the seasoning mixture onto the pan and mix well so that all the vegetables and tofu are well coated.
8. Adjust the flavor with salt and black pepper to taste.

9. Transfer the tofu and vegetables to a serving platter and garnish with toasted sesame seeds.
10. Serve your tofu stir- fried fry with side dishes of low-carb vegetables or quinoa to maintain block balance.
11. This recipe offers a protein-rich option for Zone Diet followers, with the versatility of tofu and the goodness of mixed greens. Adjust portions according to your individual nutritional needs.

Spicy Minced Chicken With Mango

Ingredients:

- 0.5C152 grams of cauliflower rice
- 1.25C17 grams of (brown) rice
- 0.5C59 grams of onion
- 1F3 grams of olive oil
- 3F9 grams of cashew nuts
- 4P132 grams of minced chicken
- 1.25C83 grams of mango
- 0.5C143 grams of cucumber
- Half a red pepper

Directions:
1. Dice the onions, the mango, the cumcumber and the red pepper.

2. In one pan add the onions, some garlic & the olive oil and bake for a couple of minutes.
3. In another pan mix the cauliflower rice, the brown rice, a chicken stock cube, some curry (masala) spices.
4. Add boiled water until almost everything is covered by it. Cook with a lid on top of it on medium fire.
5. Add the minced chicken to the onions and add some salt & pepper, coriander and the diced red peppers.
6. When the chicken is baked add the cucumber and mango and put it on low heat.
7. The rice is cooked when the liquid is gone. It will take about 15-20 minutes.
8. After plating it up together add the cashews and enjoy.

Chicken Summer Rolls

Ingredients:

- 0.25C72 grams of cucumber
- 0.25C34 grams of taugé
- 1C40 grams of noodles
- 3F30 grams of avocado
- 1F3 grams of sesame seeds
- 4P132 grams of chicken breast
- 2C24 grams of rice paper (3 pieces)
- 0.25C57 grams of bell pepper
- 0.25C33 grams of carrot
- half a red pepper

Directions:

1. Chop the chicken breast into pieces and mix them with some soy sauce, ginger, lime juice, pepper, cumin and salt.
2. Slice all the vegetables into small strips. (Cucumber, bell pepper, carrot and avocado).
3. You can dice the red pepper into small pieces.
4. Bake the chicken pieces and put them in a bowl.
5. Put all the ingredients into seperate bowls. (including the taugé and sesame seeds)
6. If your noodles need cooking first do so before putting them in a bowl.
7. Pour some hot water into a large bowl, large enough to fit a rice paper sheet.
8. Put a rice paper sheet into the bowl until it's soft, take it out and put it on a plate.
9. It's a bit tricky to get the rice paper unbroken & unfolded on a plate, but you'll get the hang of it.

10. Put the different Ingredients:a little out of the middle on the rice paper sheet.
11. Wrap the sides closed first.Then the smaller length part. Wrap the other part around it as tightly as you can.
12. For the dressing I mixed soy sauce with lime juice, pepper, ginger and cumin.

Vanilla Strawberry Doughnuts

Ingredients:

- 1 tsp baking soda
- 136g all-purpose flour
- 2 tsp vanilla
- 2 tbsp butter, melted
- 73g sugar
- 1 egg
- ½ cup strawberries, diced
- 80ml cup milk
- 1 tsp cinnamon
- ½ tsp salt

Directions:

1. In a bowl, mix flour, cinnamon, baking soda, sugar, and salt.
2. In a separate bowl, whisk egg, milk, butter, and vanilla.
3. Pour egg mixture into the flour mixture and mix until well combined.
4. Add strawberries and mix well.
5. Pour batter into the silicone doughnut moulds.
6. Insert a crisper plate in the Ninja Foodi air fryer baskets.
7. Place doughnut moulds in both baskets.
8. Select zone 1, then select "air fry" mode and set the temperature to 320 degrees F for 15 minutes. Press "match" to match zone 2 settings to zone 1. Press "start/stop" to begin.

Sausage Breakfast Casserole

Ingredients:

- 1 green capsicum diced
- 1 red capsicum diced
- 1 yellow capsicum diced
- ¼ cup sweet onion diced
- 455g hash browns
- 455g ground breakfast sausage
- 4 eggs

Directions:

1. Layer each air fryer basket with parchment paper.
2. Place the hash browns in both the baskets.
3. Spread sausage, onion and peppers over the hash brown.

4. Return the air fryer basket 1 to Zone 1, and basket 2 to Zone 2 of the Ninja Foodi 2-Basket Air Fryer.
5. Choose the "Air Fry" mode for Zone 1 at 355 degrees F temperature and 10 minutes of cooking time.
6. Select the "MATCH COOK" option to copy the settings for Zone 2.
7. Initiate cooking by pressing the START/PAUSE BUTTON.
8. Beat eggs in a bowl and pour over the air fried veggies.
9. Continue air frying for 10 minutes.
10. Garnish with salt and black pepper.
11. Serve warm.

Lentil Soup

Ingredients:

- 4 cups vegetable broth
- 1 bay leaf
- 1 teaspoon ground cumin
- 1/2 teaspoon paprika
- Salt and pepper to taste
- Fresh parsley, chopped (for garnish)
- 1 cup dried lentils
- 1 onion, diced
- 2 carrots, diced
- 2 celery stalks, diced
- 2 cloves garlic, minced

Directions:

1. Rinse the lentils under cold water and drain.
2. In a large pot, heat olive oil over medium heat.
3. Add onion, carrots, celery, and garlic. Sauté until vegetables are tender.
4. Add lentils, vegetable broth, bay leaf, cumin, and paprika to the pot.
5. Bring the soup to a boil, then reduce heat to low and simmer for 25-30 minutes, until the lentils are cooked and tender.
6. Season with salt and pepper to taste.
7. Remove the bay leaf before serving.
8. Garnish with fresh parsley.

Baked Salmon With Lemon And Dill

Ingredients:

- 4 salmon fillets
- 2 lemons, sliced
- 4 sprigs fresh dill
- 2 tablespoons olive oil
- Salt and pepper to taste

Directions:
1. Preheat the oven to 375°F (190°C).
2. Place salmon fillets on a baking sheet lined with parchment paper.
3. Drizzle olive oil over the salmon fillets.
4. Season with salt and pepper.
5. Place lemon slices and fresh dill on top of each fillet.

6. Bake in the preheated oven for 12-15 minutes, until the salmon is cooked through and flakes easily with a fork.
7. Serve hot.

Umibudo, Additionally Referred To As Sea Grape Salad

Ingredients:

- A serving of soy sauce
- 1 teaspoon of sugar
- 1 tablespoon of vinegar (apple cider vinegar or rice vinegar)
- 1 clean umibudo (sea grape) bunch
- Sesame seeds, if preferred

Directions:
1. Very well rinse and drain the ocean grapes.
2. To create the dressing, combine the soy sauce, vinegar, and sugar in a small bowl.
3. Integrate the dressing with the ocean grapes.
4. If desired, pinnacle with sesame seeds.
5. provide a cool aspect dish.

6. Those traditional Okinawan dishes highlight the unique components discovered on the island, including bitter melon, tofu, and sea grapes.
7. Experience these foods to enjoy the numerous flavors and wealthy cultural legacy of Okinawan cuisine.

Rafute Miso

Ingredients:

- 2 teaspoons of candy rice wine called mirin
- 2/fourths cup soy sauce
- 1 cup of water
- 2 chopped garlic cloves
- 1 piece of ginger (approximately 2 inches)
- Cubed 1.five lbs. (700g) of beef stomach
- half a cup of miso paste in crimson
- quarter cup brown sugar
- Sake (rice wine), 1/4 cup
- Cooking oil

Directions:

1. Heat a small amount of cooking oil to medium-excessive heat in a large saucepan or Dutch oven.
2. Upload the cubes of beef belly and brown them throughout.
3. If essential, trim the extra fat.
4. Stir in the minced garlic and the ginger slices, and cook for one minute, or until fragrant.
5. To make the braising sauce, integrate the pink miso paste, brown sugar, sake, mirin, soy sauce, and water in a separate bowl.
6. Cover the beef in the saucepan with the sauce.
7. Bring to a boil, cover, and simmer for about an hour on low heat, or till the pork is cooked and the sauce is thick. Serve with steaming rice.

Goya Chanpuru Tofu, Or "Sour Melon And Tofu Stir-Fry"

Ingredients:

- A serving of soy sauce
- A serving of miso paste
- Cooking oil, one teaspoon
- Pepper and salt as favored
- 1 deseeded and thinly sliced bitter melon (goya)
- 1 cubed piece of firm tofu
- Half of a finely sliced onion
- 2 minced garlic cloves

Directions:
1. (Soaking sour melon, then sautéing garlic, onions, and tofu) as in the Goya Champuru recipe.
2. Incorporate soy sauce and miso paste nicely in a small bowl.

3. Pour the sauce over the stir-fry, coating all of the Ingredients:.
4. Hold stirring until the tofu is cooked through and the sour melon is tender.
5. five. To taste, add salt and pepper to the food.
6. Serve hot with steamed rice.

Spinach And Feta Cheese Muffins:

Ingredients:

- 1 cup packed fresh spinach, finely chopped
- 1/2 cup crumbled feta cheese
- 1/4 cup chopped green onions
- 1 cup milk of your choice
- 1/4 cup olive oil
- 1 1/2 cups whole wheat flour
- 2 teaspoons baking powder
- 1/2 teaspoon salt
- 1/4 teaspoon black pepper
- 2 large eggs

Directions:

1. Preheat the oven to 375°F (190°C) and line a muffin tin with paper liners.
2. In a large bowl, whisk together the whole wheat flour, baking powder, salt, and black pepper.
3. Add the chopped spinach, crumbled feta cheese, and chopped green onions to the dry Ingredients:. Stir to combine.
4. In a separate bowl, whisk together the milk, olive oil, and eggs.
5. Pour the wet Ingredients:into the dry Ingredients:and stir until just combined. Do not overmix.
6. Divide the batter evenly among the prepared muffin cups.
7. Bake for 18-20 minutes, or until a toothpick inserted into the center of a muffin comes out clean.

8. Allow the muffins to cool in the pan for a few minutes, then transfer them to a wire rack to cool completely.

Overnight Oats With Almond Milk, Chia Seeds, And Sliced Peaches:

Ingredients:

- 1 tablespoon chia seeds
- 1/2 cup almond milk (or any milk of your choice)
- 1/2 cup sliced peaches (fresh or frozen)
- 1/2 cup rolled oats
- Optional toppings: honey, nuts, cinnamon

Directions:
1. In a jar or container with a lid, combine the rolled oats, chia seeds, and almond milk.
2. Stir well to ensure the oats and chia seeds are fully submerged in the almond milk.
3. Add the sliced peaches to the mixture.
4. Cover the jar or container with a lid and refrigerate overnight, or for at least 6 hours.

5. In the morning, give the overnight oats a good stir.
6. If desired, drizzle with honey, sprinkle with nuts or cinnamon, and enjoy.

Ikarian Herb Omelette

Ingredients:

- 1/4 cup onion, finely chopped
- 1/4 cup red bell pepper, finely chopped
- 1 tablespoon olive oil
- Salt and pepper to taste
- 3 large eggs
- 1/4 cup fresh mixed herbs (such as parsley, dill, mint, and oregano), finely chopped
- Optional: Crumbled feta cheese for extra flavor

Directions:

1. Prepare the Herbs: Wash and finely chop a mix of fresh herbs like parsley, dill, mint, and oregano. You can adjust the herbs and their quantities based on your taste preferences.

2. Whisk the Eggs: Crack the eggs into a bowl and whisk them until the yolks and whites are well combined. Season the eggs with a pinch of salt and some freshly ground black pepper.
3. Sauté the Onion and Pepper: Heat the olive oil in a non-stick skillet over medium heat. Add the finely chopped onion and red bell pepper. Sauté them until they become soft and translucent, which should take about 3-5 minutes.
4. Add the Herbs: Stir in the chopped fresh herbs and cook for an additional 1-2 minutes. The herbs should release their aroma and become fragrant.
5. Pour in the Eggs: Pour the beaten eggs evenly over the sautéed vegetables and herbs in the skillet. Swirl the pan to ensure an even distribution of the mixture.
6. Cook the Omelette: Allow the omelette to cook undisturbed for a few minutes until the

edges start to set and the bottom becomes golden brown. You can use a spatula to lift the edges and let the uncooked egg flow to the edges.

7. Optional Feta Cheese: If you like, sprinkle crumbled feta cheese over one half of the omelette at this point for an extra layer of flavor.
8. Fold and Serve: Once the omelette is mostly set but still slightly runny on top, carefully fold it in half using a spatula. Press down gently to seal the omelette.
9. Plate and Enjoy: Slide the Ikarian Herb Omelette onto a plate and serve hot. It's a nutritious and flavorful breakfast option inspired by the Mediterranean diet, known for its health benefits.

Vegetable Scramble

Ingredients:

- 1/4 cup diced zucchini
- 1/4 cup chopped spinach or kale
- 2 tablespoons feta cheese (optional)
- 2 tablespoons olive oil
- 1/2 teaspoon dried oregano
- Salt and pepper to taste
- 4 large eggs
- 1/2 cup diced tomatoes
- 1/2 cup diced bell peppers (red, gree, or a mix of colors)
- 1/4 cup diced red onion
- Fresh basil leaves for garnish (optional)

Directions:

1. Prepare the Vegetables: Start by chopping all the vegetables into small, uniform pieces to ensure even cooking.
2. Heat the Olive Oil: In a non-stick skillet, heat the olive oil over medium heat.
3. Saute the Onion and Peppers: Add the diced red onion and bell peppers to the skillet. Saute them for about 3-4 minutes until they start to soften and become slightly translucent.
4. Add the Zucchini and Tomatoes: Add the diced zucchini and tomatoes to the skillet. Continue cooking for another 3-4 minutes until the zucchini begins to soften, and the tomatoes release their juices.
5. Toss in Spinach or Kale: Add the chopped spinach or kale to the skillet and stir it into the mixture. Cook for an additional 2-3 minutes until the greens wilt.

6. Season and Spice: Sprinkle dried oregano, salt, and pepper over the vegetable mixture. Stir well to distribute the seasonings evenly.
7. Scramble the Eggs: In a separate bowl, whisk the eggs until the yolks and whites are well combined.
8. Combine Eggs and Vegetables: Pour the beaten eggs over the sauteed vegetables in the skillet. Stir gently and continuously to scramble the eggs and combine them with the vegetables. Cook until the eggs are fully set but still moist.
9. Optional Feta Cheese: If you like, sprinkle crumbled feta cheese over the scramble. It adds a creamy and salty element to the dish.
10. Garnish and Serve: Once the eggs are cooked to your desired consistency, remove the skillet from the heat. Garnish with fresh basil leaves if available.

11. Plate and Enjoy: Your Mediterranean Vegetable Scramble is ready to be served. It's a flavorful and healthy breakfast option inspired by Mediterranean cuisine.

Arroz Con Pollo

Ingredients:

- 1/4 cup water
- 4 oz vegetable broth
- 1/2 bay leaves
- 1/2 tsp oregano (dried)
- 1 1/2 cup green beans (frozen and thawed, chopped)
- 1/2 cup chicken breast meat (perdue brand short cuts)
- salt and pepper (to taste)
- 1/2 cup zone pastarx orzo
- 1 tsp olive oil
- 1/2 medium onion (finely chopped)

- 1 clove garlic (minced)
- 1/4 cup tomato sauce
- 2 tsp dr. sears' zone extra virgin olive oil

Directions:

1. Prepare Zone PastaRx Orzo according to package Directions:. Set aside.
2. Meanwhile, warm 1 teaspoon oil in a large skillet over medium to high heat. When hot, add the onion and garlic and cook for 2 to 3 minutes, or until just golden.
3. Add the tomato sauce, water, broth, bay leaves, oregano, salt and pepper. Stir well and bring to a boil.
4. Add the green beans, stir well, cover, and simmer for about 8 minutes.
5. Add the cooked orzo and chicken to warm, and cook another 2 minutes.
6. To serve, drizzle each serving with 1 teaspoon of extra virgin olive oil.

Chicken Stir Fry

Ingredients:

- 3/4 cup Water chestnuts (sliced)
- 8 oz Mushrooms (sliced)
- 1 Red bell pepper (sliced)
- 1 cup Snow peas
- 1/2 cup Scallions (sliced)
- 2 tsps Low sodium soy sauce
- 1/2 cup Mandarin orange sections
- 3 cups Broccoli (chopped)
- 2 tsps Dr. Sears' Zone Extra Virgin Olive Oil
- 7 oz Boneless skinless chicken breast (cut into bite sized pieces)
- 2 cloves Garlic (pressed)

- 1 tsp Toasted sesame oil

Directions:

1. Steam the broccoli for 3-4 minutes, rinse with cold water to stop cooking. Set aside to drain in colander.
2. Heat the olive oil In a large skillet to medium.
3. Add chicken and garlic, cook until juices run clear.
4. Add water chestnuts, mushrooms, pepper, snow peas, scallions and soy sauce.
5. Cook until tender (add vegetable stock in tablespoon increments, if needed).
6. Stir in the mandarin orange sections and toasted sesame oil. Serve.

Baby Spinach And Strawberry Salad

Ingredients:

Salad:

- 1/4 Red Onion - thinly sliced
- 10 Strawberries - sliced
- 1/4 cup Garbanzo beans canned - rinsed/drained
- 1/3 cup Cooked skinless chicken breast cut into bite-sized pieces (Leftovers or Perdue Short Cuts)
- 3 cups Baby spinach - tear stems off
- 1 cup Portobello mushrooms - chopped

Dressing:

- 1/4 tsp Grated orange zest
- 1/4 tsp Sea salt

- 1/8 tsp Ground black pepper
- 1 tbsp Fresh squeezed orange juice
- 1 1/2 tsps Dr. Sears' Zone Extra Virgin Olive Oil
- 1 tsp Shallot - 1 minced (one heaping tablespoon)
- 1 tbsp Champagne vinegar

Directions:
1. Wash spinach and spin dry. Place in a large bowl with remaining salad ingredients.
2. Heat a small skillet over medium-low heat. Add olive oil, shallot, champagne vinegar, orange zest, salt and pepper. Cook until shallot is translucent, 2-3 minutes.
3. Whisk in orange juice.
4. Drizzle warm dressing over salad mixture.
5. Toss gently to wilt spinach.

Eggplant Caviar

Ingredients:

- 2 cloves garlic - minced
- 1 tbsp fresh squeezed lemon juice
- 1/2 tsp dried basil leaves
- 2 tbsps kitchen basics unsalted vegetable stock
- Black pepper
- 2 1/2 lbs eggplants - same size
- 1/2 cup scallions - minced
- 2 1/2 tsps dr. Sears' zone extra virgin olive oil

Directions:

1. Preheat oven to 400° F (or grill).
2. Cut eggplants in half length-wise and place on a baking sheet with their cut-sides facing

down. Bake for 20 minutes or until they are fork-tender.
3. Remove the pulp from the skin and puree in a food processor or blender.
4. Add remaining ingredients except olive oil and blend well.
5. Stir in olive oil.
6. Serve at room temperature or chill for 1 hour.

Dill Sauce

Ingredients:

- 3/4 tsp dr. sears' zone extra virgin olive oil
- 1 tsp garlic - minced
- 1 tsp dill
- 1 1/2 tsps cornstarch
- 1/3 cup 0%-fat greek yogurt
- 2 tsp dry white wine
- salt and pepper - to taste

Directions:

1. In a small saucepan combine yogurt, white wine, olive oil, garlic, and dill. Turn the heat to low. Do not boil.
2. Make a slurry (thin paste) by combining the cornstarch with a little water.

3. Whisk the cornstarch mixture into the yogurt, stirring often. Bring to a simmer (that's when the sauce will thicken) and then return heat to very low. Do not boil.

Brazilian Tilapia Stew

Ingredients:

- 12 ounces of tilapia, cut into pieces about 2-inches large

For the marinade:

- Juice from 1 lime, at least 2 tablespoons
- 3/4 tablespoon olive oil
- 3 garlic cloves, minced
- 1 1/2 tablespoons minced ginger
- 1 green onion, minced
- 2 tablespoons chopped cilantro

For the stew:

- 3/4 teaspoon olive oil

- 1 each: medium-sized bell pepper and onion, diced
- 2 tablespoons each: minced garlic and ginger
- 2 tablespoons chopped cilantro
- 1 bottle (8-ounces) clam juice
- 1 bay leaf
- 1 cup seafood or vegetable stock
- 1 cup lite coconut milk
- 2 tablespoons tomato paste
- 2 diced tomatoes
- Salt and pepper to taste

Directions:

Marinate the tilapia:

1. Combine all the marinade Ingredients:together in a tightly covered bowl

or sealable bag; add the tilapia pieces to the marinade and refrigerate for 30 minutes.
2. Heat the olive oil in a heavy saucepan to medium heat; add the pepper and onion; cook for 5 minutes or until soft.
3. Add the remaining Ingredients:, except the tomatoes and tilapia, to the pot and bring to a boil; reduce the heat and simmer for 10 minutes.
4. Add the tilapia and cook for another 3 minutes or until done. Stir the tomatoes into the pot and cook for about 2 minutes or until warmed throughout.

Bella Buns With Tuna Burgers

Ingredients:

For the tuna burgers:

- 1/2 cup finely chopped celery
- 1/3 cup bell pepper, finely chopped
- 2 teaspoons olive oil
- 4 cleaned portabella mushroom caps
- 1 can (6 ounces) chunk tuna in water, drained well
- 1 egg white
- 2 tablespoons rolled oats, not the quick cooking variety
- 1 tablespoon chili sauce
- 1/2 teaspoon each: hot sauce and Worcestershire sauce

For the spread:

- 1 cup garden salad of choice
- 1/2 medium apple
- 1 1/2 tablespoons low-fat mayonnaise
- 1 tablespoon plain low-fat yogurt
- 1 teaspoon dill weed
- Sliced tomato, onion and lettuce
- 1 dill pickle spear

Directions:

1. Mix all the burger Ingredients:together, except the olive oil and mushrooms; form the mixture into 2 patties. Cook the patties for 4 minutes per side or until cooked through.
2. Grill the mushroom caps in the same pan for 1 minute per side.

Make the spread:

3. Combine all the Ingredients:listed for the spread and mix well.

Assemble the burger:

4. Spread equal amounts of the mayonnaise mixture on each mushroom cap; layer the burger followed by the desired condiments using the mushrooms as a bun.

Scrambled Eggs With Spinach And Tomatoes

Ingredients:

- 1 medium tomato, diced
- 1 teaspoon olive oil
- Salt and black pepper
- 2 eggs
- 1 cup fresh spinach, washed and chopped
- Fresh herbs (parsley, basil) for garnish (optional)

Directions:
1. In a nonstick skillet, heat the olive oil over medium heat.
2. Add the chopped spinach and cook until slightly wilted.
3. Add the diced tomatoes to the pan and cook for another 2-3 minutes.

4. Beat the eggs in a bowl and pour them into the pan with the spinach and tomatoes.
5. Gently mix the eggs with the Ingredients:in the pan until they are fully cooked.
6. Add salt and black pepper to taste.
7. Serve the scrambled eggs on a serving platter.
8. Garnish with fresh herbs if desired.
9. Accompany eggs with a serving of leafy greens or a low-carb option to maintain block balance.
10. This scrambled egg recipe is a delicious, protein-packed option for breakfast or lunch. Adjust portions based on your individual nutritional needs.

Tuna Salad With Chickpeas And Cherry Tomatoes

Ingredients:

- 1 cup cherry tomatoes, cut in half
- 1 tablespoon olive oil
- Juice of 1/2 lemon
- Salt and black pepper
- 1 can tuna in oil, drained
- 1/2 cup cooked chickpeas
- Fresh basil leaves for garnish (optional)

Directions:

1. In a bowl, combine the drained tuna in oil, the cooked chickpeas and the cherry tomatoes cut in half.
2. Add the olive oil and lemon juice to the bowl. Mix well to distribute the seasonings.

3. Adjust the flavor with salt and black pepper to taste.
4. Leave the salad in the refrigerator for at least 15-20 minutes to allow the flavors to blend.
5. Before serving, garnish with fresh basil leaves if desired.
6. Serve the tuna salad with chickpeas and cherry tomatoes on a bed of lettuce or leafy greens to keep the blocks balanced.
7. This tuna salad is a high-protein option packed with fresh flavors. Adjust portions based on your individual nutritional needs.

Turkey Burger With Guacamole

Ingredients:

- Salt and black pepper
- 1/2 ripe avocado
- 1/4 red onion, finely chopped
- 1 tomato, thinly sliced
- Lettuce leaves for assembly
- 150g of minced turkey meat
- 1 tablespoon red onion, finely chopped
- 1 teaspoon mustard
- 1 teaspoon low-sodium soy sauce
- 1 wholemeal roll or a lettuce leaf to serve

Directions:

For the Turkey Burgers:

1. In a bowl, mix the ground turkey with the chopped red onion, mustard, soy sauce, salt and pepper.
2. Divide the mixture in two and form two burgers.
3. Cook the burgers in a non-stick pan or on the grill for about 5-7 minutes per side or until cooked through.

For the Guacamole:

4. Mash the avocado pulp in a bowl.
5. Add the chopped red onion and mix well.
6. Adjust the flavor with salt and black pepper to taste.

Assembly:

7. Place the cooked turkey burger on a whole-wheat bun or lettuce leaf.
8. Add a generous portion of guacamole on top of the burger.
9. Add tomato slices and lettuce leaves.

10. Close with another layer of sandwich or another lettuce leaf, depending on your preferences.
11. Serve the turkey burger with guacamole with vegetable-based sides or a serving of leafy greens to keep the blocks balanced.
12. This recipe offers a delicious turkey burger alternative with a healthy twist thanks to guacamole. Adjust portions based on your individual nutritional needs.

Grilled Polenta With Ham & Asperagus

Ingredients:

- 1.5P32 grams of parmasan cheese
- 2.5P73 grams of smoked ham
- 3.75C44 grams of polenta (cornmeal)
- 0.25C125 grams of asperagus
- 2F4 grams of pesto
- 2F4 grams of butter

Directions:
1. Add a half a stock cube to 225ml boiling water.
2. Add the polenta bit by bit and stir well.
3. Add the butter and make sure it's dissolved completely.
4. Take the pan of the stove in mix in the cheese, some salt & pepper and (fresh) basil.

5. Add a waxpaper sheet to a baking tin and pour the mixture into it.
6. Let it set for an hour.
7. In the mean time clean the asperagus (cut off the bottoms) and grill them in the oven for about 20 minutes.
8. Cut the polenta in slices and grill them for a couple of minutes.
9. Serve the slices with pesto and ham next to the asperagus.

Noodles With Chicken & Brussel Sprouts

Ingredients:

- 1.25C218 grams of brussel sprouts
- 0.75C174 grams of bell pepper
- 1F2 grams of olive oil
- 4P136 grams of (veggie) chicken
- 2C80 grams of noodles
- 3F9 grams of sesame seeds

Directions:

1. Cut up the (veggie) chicken if needed and season any way you like.
2. Clean the brussel sprouts and cut them in half.
3. Dice the bell pepper in small pieces.
4. Bake the chicken in olive oil and add my go-to seasoning: salt, pepper, soy sauce, ginger, coriander and cumin.

5. Add the veggies and bake until they're cooked.
6. If needed cook the noodles first then add them to the pan.
7. Serve with sesame seeds on top.

Egg With Baby Spinach

Ingredients:

- 2 garlic cloves, minced
- 1/3 teaspoon kosher salt
- 6-8 large eggs
- ½ cup half and half
- Salt and black pepper, to taste
- Nonstick spray, for greasing ramekins
- 2 tablespoons olive oil
- 6 ounces baby spinach
- 8 Sourdough bread slices, toasted

Directions:

1. Grease 4 ramekins with oil spray and set aside for further use.
2. Take a skillet and heat oil in it.

3. Then cook spinach for 2 minutes and add garlic and salt black pepper.
4. Let it simmer for2more minutes.
5. Once the spinach is wilted, transfer it to a plate.
6. Whisk an egg into a small bowl.
7. Add in the spinach.
8. Whisk it well and then pour half and half.
9. Divide this mixture between 4 ramekins and remember not to overfill it to the top, leave a little space on top.
10. Put the ramekins in zone 1 and zone 2 baskets of the Ninja Foodie 2-Basket Air Fryer.
11. Press start and set zone 1 to AIR fry it at 350 degrees F for 8-12 minutes.
12. Press the MATCH button for zone 2.
13. Once it's cooked and eggs are done, serve with sourdough bread slices.

Frittata

Ingredients:

- 15g spinach chopped
- 1 tablespoon fresh herbs, chopped
- 2 spring onion chopped
- Salt and black pepper, to taste
- 4 eggs
- 4 tablespoons milk
- 35g cheddar cheese grated
- 50g feta crumbled
- 1 tomato, deseeded and chopped
- ½ teaspoon olive oil

Directions:

1. Beat eggs with milk in a bowl and stir in the rest of the Ingredients:.
2. Grease two small-sized springform pans and line them with parchment paper.
3. Divide the egg mixture into the pans and place one in each air fryer basket.
4. Return the air fryer basket 1 to Zone 1, and basket 2 to Zone 2 of the Ninja Foodi 2-Basket Air Fryer.
5. Choose the "Air Fry" mode for Zone 1 at 350 degrees F and 12 minutes of cooking time.
6. Select the "MATCH COOK" option to copy the settings for Zone 2.
7. Initiate cooking by pressing the START/PAUSE BUTTON.
8. Serve warm.

Sweet Potato And Black Bean Tacos

Ingredients:

- 1/2 teaspoon ground cumin
- 1/2 teaspoon paprika
- Salt and pepper to taste
- 1 can black beans, rinsed and drained
- 1/2 cup diced tomatoes
- 1/4 cup chopped cilantro
- 2 sweet potatoes, peeled and diced
- 1 tablespoon olive oil
- 1 teaspoon chili powder
- Corn tortillas

Directions:

1. Preheat the oven to 425°F (220°C).

2. In a bowl, toss sweet potatoes with olive oil, chili powder, cumin, paprika, salt, and pepper until well coated.
3. Spread the seasoned sweet potatoes on a baking sheet and bake for 20-25 minutes, until tender and lightly browned.
4. In a small bowl, combine black beans, diced tomatoes, and chopped cilantro.
5. Warm corn tortillas in a dry skillet over medium heat.
6. Fill each tortilla with roasted sweet potatoes and the black bean mixture.
7. Add optional toppings if desired. Serve warm.

Grilled Chicken

Ingredients:

- 2 tablespoons olive oil
- 2 cloves garlic, minced
- 1 teaspoon dried oregano
- 1/2 teaspoon dried thyme
- Salt and pepper to taste
- 4 chicken breasts
- 1 lemon, juiced

Directions:

1. In a bowl, whisk together lemon juice, olive oil, minced garlic, dried oregano, dried thyme, salt, and pepper.
2. Place chicken breasts in a shallow dish and pour the marinade over them. Ensure the chicken is well coated.

3. Cover the dish and marinate in the refrigerator for at least 1 hour or overnight.
4. Preheat a grill or grill pan over medium-high heat.
5. Remove the chicken from the marinade and discard the excess marinade.
6. Grill the chicken breasts for about 6-7 minutes per side, until cooked through and no longer pink in the center.
7. Allow the chicken to rest for a few minutes before slicing.
8. Serve hot.

Shima Rakkyo

Ingredients:

- 1 cup of rice vinegar
- 1/eight teaspoon salt
- 1/2 lb. wiped-clean and peeled Okinawan shallots (Rakkyo)
- 1/2 cup sugar

Directions:

1. Incorporate rice vinegar, sugar, and salt in a small pot.
2. Bring to a boil while stirring to completely dissolve the sugar.
3. Place the shallots in a clean glass jar after peeling them.
4. Cover the shallots with the recent vinegar aggregate.

5. After the jar is sealed, let it reach room temperature.
6. Store within the refrigerator for no less than an afternoon before serving. Over the years, the pickled shallots will take on a sweet and tart taste.
7. Those new Okinawan dishes contribute to the diverse tapestry of Okinawan cuisine with the aid of substances like red meat stomach, miso, and rakkyo (Okinawan shallots). experience coming across these recipes and tasting Okinawa's extraordinary tastes.

Goya Miso

Ingredients:

- 1 sour melon (goya), thinly sliced and deseeded
- 2 teaspoons of mirin (candy rice wine)
- 2 tbsp. sake (rice wine)
- 2 tablespoons of red or white miso paste
- 1 tablespoon each of sugar and frying oil
  Sesame seeds as an elective garnish

Directions:

1. To make the miso sauce, mix the miso paste, mirin, sake, and sugar in a small basin.
2. In a pan, warm the frying oil to a medium-high temperature.
3. Stir-fry the sliced bitter melon for a couple of minutes until it starts to soften.

4. After uniformly coating the bitter melon, drizzle the miso sauce over it.
5. Retain stir-frying until the sauce thickens and the sour melon is tender.
6. If favored, upload sesame seeds as a garnish.
7. Combine with steaming rice as a side dish.

Somen Chanpuru

Ingredients:

- 2 minced garlic cloves

- 2 teaspoons of soy sauce

- 1 tsp. mirin (candy rice wine)

- 1 tablespoon of oil for cooking

- Eight ounces of somen noodles (or different thin noodles of your choosing)

- 1 block of diced company tofu; thinly sliced veggies (inclusive of bell peppers, carrots, and bean sprouts)

- Chopped inexperienced onions for garnish

Directions:

1. Put together the somen noodles in accordance with the Directions: on the box,

then rinse under bloodless water and set aside.
2. Warm the cooking oil over medium-high heat in a large pan or wok.
3. Include tofu cubes and minced garlic. Stir-fry the tofu until it starts to brown.
4. Include the opposite veggies and stir-fry them until they begin to melt.
5. Combine the soy sauce and mirin in a small basin, then pour the combination over the tofu and greens.
6. Encompass the cooked somen noodles and stir everything up nicely.
7. Continue to prepare dinner for a few extra minutes to absolutely reheat the noodles.
8. Add chopped inexperienced onions as a garnish and serve right away.
9. Those additional Okinawan dishes, which encompass a few noodles with veggies and sour melon with miso, offer a more

comprehensive view of the island's distinctive tastes and culinary customs.
10. Experience these recipes as you learn more about Okinawan cooking.

Sweet Potato Hash With Bell Peppers, Onions, And A Poached Egg:

Ingredients:

- 1/4 cup diced onions
- 1 teaspoon olive oil
- Salt and pepper to taste
- 1 medium sweet potato, peeled and diced
- 1/2 cup diced bell peppers
- 1 poached egg

Directions:

1. Heat olive oil in a skillet over medium heat.
2. Add the diced sweet potatoes, bell peppers, and onions to the skillet.
3. Season with salt and pepper.
4. Sauté for about 10-12 minutes until the sweet potatoes are tender and lightly browned.

5. While the hash is cooking, poach an egg separately.
6. Once the sweet potato hash is ready, transfer it to a plate and top with the poached egg.
7. Season with additional salt and pepper if desired.
8. Serve hot.

Brown Rice Cake With Almond Butter And Sliced Strawberries:

Ingredients:

- 1 brown rice cake
- 1 tablespoon almond butter (or any nut butter of your choice)
- Sliced strawberries

Directions:

1. Spread the almond butter evenly onto the brown rice cake.
2. Top with sliced strawberries.
3. Enjoy as is or drizzle with honey for added sweetness.

Whole Grain Waffles With A Side Of Greek Yogurt And Fresh Fruit:

Ingredients:

- 1/4 teaspoon salt
- 1 cup milk of your choice
- 1 tablespoon melted coconut oil or butter
- Greek yogurt
- 1 cup whole wheat flour
- 1 tablespoon coconut sugar or sweetener of your choice
- 1 teaspoon baking powder
- Fresh fruit of your choice (e.g., berries, sliced bananas, kiwi)

Directions:

1. In a bowl, whisk together the whole wheat flour, coconut sugar, baking powder, and salt.
2. Add the milk and melted coconut oil or butter to the dry Ingredients:. Stir until just combined.
3. Preheat a waffle iron and lightly coat it with cooking spray or a small amount of oil.
4. Pour the batter onto the waffle iron according to the manufacturer's Directions:.
5. Cook until golden brown and crisp.
6. Serve the whole grain waffles with a dollop of Greek yogurt and a side of fresh fruit.

Adventist Breakfast Burrito

Ingredients:

- 1/4 cup black beans (canned, rinsed, and drained)
- 1/4 cup diced avocado
- 1/4 cup shredded low-fat cheese (optional)
- 2 tablespoons salsa (mild or spicy, based on your preference)
- Salt and pepper to taste
- Cooking spray or a small amount of olive oil for the skillet
- 2 large whole wheat or whole grain tortillas
- 4 large eggs
- 1/4 cup diced bell peppers (any color)
- 1/4 cup diced onions

- 1/4 cup diced tomatoes
- Fresh cilantro or parsley for garnish (optional)

Directions:

1. Prepare the Eggs: In a bowl, crack the eggs and whisk them until the yolks and whites are well combined. Season with a pinch of salt and pepper to taste.
2. Cook the Vegetables: Heat a non-stick skillet over medium heat and lightly coat it with cooking spray or a small amount of olive oil.
3. Add the diced bell peppers and onions to the skillet and sauté for about 3-4 minutes until they begin to soften.
4. Add Tomatoes and Black Beans: Stir in the diced tomatoes and black beans with the sautéed vegetables. Cook for an additional 2-3 minutes until the tomatoes soften and the beans are heated through.
5. Scramble the Eggs: Push the vegetable mixture to one side of the skillet and pour the

beaten eggs into the empty side. Stir the eggs continuously until they are scrambled and cooked to your desired level of doneness.

6. Assemble the Burritos: Lay out the whole wheat tortillas on a clean surface. Place half of the scrambled eggs onto each tortilla, spreading them out evenly.

7. Add Avocado and Cheese: Sprinkle diced avocado and shredded low-fat cheese (if using) over the eggs.

8. Drizzle with Salsa: Spoon salsa over the top for added flavor. Adjust the amount based on your preference for spiciness.

9. Roll and Serve: Carefully fold in the sides of each tortilla and then roll it up from the bottom to create a burrito. Repeat for the second tortilla.

10. Garnish (Optional): If you like, garnish your Adventist Breakfast Burritos with fresh

cilantro or parsley for a burst of color and flavor.
11. Enjoy: Your Adventist Breakfast Burritos are now ready to be enjoyed. They are a nutritious and satisfying breakfast option, filled with protein, fiber, and healthy fats.

Japanese Miso Soup And Tofu

Ingredients:

- 1/2 cup sliced green onions (scallions)
- 1/2 cup sliced mushrooms (shiitake or white mushrooms)
- 1 sheet of nori (seaweed), cut into thin strips (optional)
- 1 teaspoon soy sauce (optional, for added flavor)
- 4 cups of water
- 2 tablespoons miso paste (white or red, based on your preference)
- 1 cup diced tofu (firm or silken, as per your preference)
- Dash of mirin (rice wine, optional)

Directions:

1. Prepare the Broth: In a medium-sized pot, bring 4 cups of water to a gentle boil. Reduce the heat to low, keeping the water at a simmer.
2. Dissolve Miso Paste: In a small bowl, whisk the miso paste with a few tablespoons of warm water to create a smooth paste. This makes it easier to incorporate into the soup without clumps.
3. Add Tofu: Carefully add the diced tofu to the simmering water. Let it simmer for about 5-7 minutes to heat through.
4. Sauté Mushrooms: In a separate pan, sauté the sliced mushrooms over medium heat until they release their moisture and become tender, which should take about 5 minutes.
5. Combine Ingredients: Once the tofu is heated through, add the dissolved miso paste to the

pot, stirring gently to combine. Make sure the miso paste is well incorporated into the broth.

6. Add Mushrooms: Add the sautéed mushrooms to the soup. Stir them in.
7. Season (Optional): If desired, add a dash of soy sauce and mirin to enhance the flavor of the soup. Adjust the seasonings to your taste.
8. Serve: Ladle the Japanese Miso Soup into bowls. Garnish with sliced green onions and nori strips, if you like.
9. Enjoy: Your Japanese Miso Soup with Tofu is now ready to be enjoyed. It's a comforting and nutritious soup often served as an appetizer in Japanese cuisine.

Baked Avocado Chicken And Vegetables

Ingredients:

- 1 cup Zucchini, sliced
- 1 cup Sliced mushrooms
- 1/2 cup Onions - chopped
- 3/4 cup Green beans
- 1/4 cup Kitchen Basics unsalted vegetable stock
- 1 (14.5 oz) can Diced tomatoes - with juice
- 2 tsp Dried basil
- 1 tbsp Avocado
- 1 tbsp Low-fat cream cheese
- 3 oz Boneless skinless chicken breast - slice to make a pocket

- Salt and pepper - to taste
- Cooking spray - olive oil
- 1 tsp Dr. Sears' Zone Extra Virgin Olive Oil - drizzle

Directions:

1. Mash the avocado and mix it with the cream cheese.
2. Slice the chicken to make a pocket.
3. Put the cream cheese/avocado mixture into this pocket and seal with a toothpick.
4. Put chicken in a baking tray and spray with olive-oil cooking spray.
5. Sprinkle with salt and pepper.
6. Bake for 20-25 minutes at 350º F.
7. Spray a skillet with olive- oil spray.
8. Sauté vegetables in 2 tablespoons of vegetable stock (more if needed) until crisp tender.
9. Add diced tomatoes and heat through.

10. Serve the vegetables in a bowl drizzled with extra virgin olive oil.
11. Place the chicken on a separate dish and enjoy your dinner.

Bbq Salmon & Brussels Orzo

Ingredients:

- 1/2 tsp smoked paprika
- 1 tsp olive oil
- 1 1/2 oz salmon
- chives (snipped, to taste)
- 1/4 cup zone pastarx orzo
- 1/2 lb brussels sprouts (quartered)
- cooking spray-olive oil pam
- 1/2 tsp garlic powder
- 1/2 tsp onion powder

Directions:
1. Prepare Zone PastaRx Orzo according to package Directions:.
2. Preheat oven to 450°F.

3. Meanwhile, spray a large rimmed baking sheet, with olive oil Pam.
4. Add Brussels sprouts and spray them with olive oil Pam, sprinkle with salt and pepper and roast for 25 minutes.
5. Mix together garlic powder, onion powder, smoked paprika and olive oil to make a sauce for the salmon.
6. Arrange salmon skin side down on baking sheet and brush with sauce.
7. Roast salmon with Brussels sprouts for 5 minutes or until sprouts are tender and salmon is cooked through, stirring sprouts halfway through.
8. Mix Brussels sprouts with orzo, place Salmon on top and sprinkle with chives.

Baked Chicken And Broccoli Salad

Ingredients:

- 1 tbsp Sesame seeds - toasted if you want

- 1/2 cup 0%-fat Greek yogurt

- 2 tsps Light mayonnaise, Hellman's

- 1 tbsp Fresh squeezed lemon juice

- 1/2 tsp Garlic powder

- Black pepper to taste

- 4 oz Boneless skinless chicken breast - (or 3 oz leftover)

- 4 slices Louis Rich turkey bacon

- 5 cups Broccoli - floret and stems chopped small

- 3 oz Water chestnuts canned - sliced and chopped

- 1/3 cup Carrots - shredded

- 1 1/2 cups Peaches canned in water, drained

Directions:

1. Preheat oven to 375°F.
2. Wash and pat chicken dry.
3. Put in a small baking dish and season with your favorite herbs. Bake for 30-35 minutes (until juices run clear).
4. Meanwhile cook bacon in microwave oven and set aside to drain and cool.
5. In a good-sized bowl mix broccoli, water chestnuts, carrots, and sesame seeds.
6. In a separate bowl mix yogurt, mayonnaise, lemon juice, garlic powder and pepper.
7. Add to vegetable mixture with cooled chicken and peaches.
8. Toss to coat. Top with crushed bacon.

Cottage Cheese With Tomato & Guac

Ingredients:

- 3 tbsp low-fat cottage cheese
- 2 tomatoes (cut in wedges)
- 1 tbsp guacamole
- Salt and pepper (to taste)

Directions:
1. Place cottage cheese in the center of a salad-sized plate.
2. Arrange tomato wedges around cottage cheese.
3. Top cottage cheese with guacamole.

Cottage Cheese Snack

Ingredients:

- 1/4 cup low-fat cottage cheese
- 1/4 tsp dried basil
- 1/4 tsp pepper
- 10 cherry tomatoes (quartered)
- 2 1/2 tbsp olives (sliced)

Directions:

1. Cut the cherry tomatoes in half.
2. Put the cottage cheese in a small bowl and stir in the basil and pepper.
3. Gently stir in the sliced olives and tomatoes.

Warm Shrimp Salad

Ingredients:

- 3/4 cup chicken stock, low-sodium
- 3 cups fresh green beans with ends removed
- 1 teaspoon each: dried basil and oregano
- 1/8 teaspoon each: thyme, cayenne pepper and ground cloves
- 6 cups of mixed salad greens
- 6 slices of tomato
- 1 tablespoon olive oil
- 3/4 cup chopped onion
- 1 minced garlic clove
- 8 ounces medium shrimp, cleaned

- 2 cups peach slices (with no added sugar, if canned)

Directions:

1. In a skillet, heat the olive oil to medium; cook the onion and garlic for 4 minutes.
2. Add the shrimp; cook and stir for 2 more minutes.
3. Stir in the remaining Ingredients:, except the salad mix, and bring to a boil. Lower the heat to simmer and cook for 5 minutes or until the shrimp are done and the green beans are crisp-tender.
4. Divide the salad greens between two plates and top each with 1/2 of the shrimp mixture.

Chicken And Applesauce Burgers

Ingredients:
For the burger:

- 1 egg white

- 2 teaspoons onion flakes, or to taste
- 1/2 teaspoon chili powder
- 3 ounces ground chicken breast
- 1/3 cup chunky applesauce, unsweetened
- 3 tablespoons old fashioned oats, not the quick cooking variety
- Spinach and Strawberry Salad with Vinaigrette Dressing (Recipe below)

Directions:
1. Preheat the broiler unit to high.
2. Mix together 1/4 cup of the applesauce, egg white, oatmeal and onions in a bowl.
3. Add the ground chicken and mix very well. Shape into one burger patty. (Note: If the mixture is too wet to easily form a patty, add some more oats until it is.)

4. Spray a pan with oil and broil the burger for 5 minutes; turn the burger over and broil for another 5 minutes or until it is done.
5. Heat the remaining applesauce and spoon over the burger or serve it on the side.

Duck Breast With Cranberry Sauce

Ingredients:

- 1/2 cup fresh or frozen cranberries
- 1 tablespoon balsamic vinegar
- 1 teaspoon honey or maple syrup (optional)
- 1 duck breast (about 200g)
- Salt and black pepper
- 1 teaspoon olive oil
- 1/4 teaspoon fresh ginger, grated

Directions:
1. Preheat the oven to 200°C.
2. Score the skin of the duck breast with a knife to form a grid. Season with salt and black pepper on both sides.
3. Heat the olive oil in a nonstick skillet over medium-high heat. Place the duck breast skin

side down and cook for about 5 minutes or until the skin is golden and crispy.
4. Transfer the duck breast to a baking tray and cook in the preheated oven for about 10-12 minutes or until cooked to your desired temperature.
5. While the duck breast cooks, prepare the cranberry sauce. In a small pot, cook cranberries with balsamic vinegar, honey (if desired), and grated ginger. Cook over medium-low heat until the blueberries break down and the sauce thickens slightly.
6. Once cooked, cut the duck breast into thin slices.
7. Serve the duck breast with the cranberry sauce on top, ensuring you maintain the balance between protein, carbohydrates and fats.
8. Accompany the dish with leafy green vegetables or other low-carb side dishes.

9. This recipe offers a delicious combination of flavors with juicy duck breast and cranberry sauce. Adjust portions based on your individual nutritional needs.

Omelette With Mushrooms And Low Fat Cheese

Ingredients:

- 2 tablespoons low-fat cheese, grated
- 1 teaspoon olive oil
- Salt and black pepper
- 2 eggs
- 1/2 cup mushrooms, sliced
- Fresh herbs (parsley, thyme) for garnish (optional)

Directions:
1. Preheat the oven to 180°C.
2. In a nonstick skillet, heat the olive oil over medium heat.
3. Add the sliced mushrooms to the pan and cook for about 3-4 minutes or until tender. Adjust the flavor with salt and black pepper.

4. In a bowl, beat the eggs and add the grated cheese. Mix well.
5. Pour the eggs and cheese over the mushrooms in the pan. Stir lightly to distribute the mushrooms evenly.
6. Cook over medium-low heat for 5 to 7 minutes or until the edges of the omelette begin to set.
7. Transfer the pan to the preheated oven and cook for an additional 5 to 7 minutes or until the omelette is cooked through and golden brown on top.
8. Once cooked, garnish with fresh herbs if desired.
9. Serve the omelette with mushrooms and cheese on a serving plate.
10. Accompany the omelet with a serving of leafy greens or a low-carb option to maintain block balance.

11. This omelette is a delicious, high-protein choice, perfect for breakfast or lunch. Adjust portions based on your individual nutritional needs.

Quinoa Salad With Chickpeas And Feta

Ingredients:

- 1 medium tomato, diced
- 1 tablespoon black olives, sliced
- 1 tablespoon olive oil
- Juice of 1/2 lemon
- Salt and black pepper
- 1/2 cup raw quinoa
- 1 cup of water
- 1/2 cup cooked chickpeas
- 50g low-fat feta, crumbled
- 1 cucumber, diced
- Fresh mint leaves for garnish (optional)

Directions:

1. Rinse the quinoa well under running water.
2. In a saucepan, bring 1 cup of water to a boil. Add the quinoa, reduce the heat and cover. Cook for about 15 minutes or until the quinoa is cooked and the water is absorbed.
3. Let the cooked quinoa cool.
4. In a large bowl, combine the cooked quinoa with the cooked chickpeas, diced cucumber, diced tomato, and sliced black olives.
5. In a small bowl, make the vinaigrette by mixing the olive oil, lemon juice, salt, and black pepper.
6. Pour the vinaigrette over the quinoa and mix well to evenly distribute the seasonings.
7. Add the crumbled feta to the quinoa and mix gently.
8. Garnish with fresh mint leaves if desired.
9. Serve quinoa salad with chickpeas and feta as a main meal or side dish.

10. Accompany the salad with a serving of leafy greens or other low-carb side dishes to maintain block balance.
11. This quinoa salad is a nutritious and tasty option, perfect for a light, balanced meal. Adjust portions based on your individual nutritional needs.

www.ingramcontent.com/pod-product-compliance
Lightning Source LLC
LaVergne TN
LVHW010222070526
838199LV00062B/4697